GOD MADE IT

The Story of Creation Told in Rhyme

Words by
Rosalind Bennett

Illustrations by
Jonathan Barnhill

Published by:
It's GiGi's World Books, LLC
itsgigisworldbooks@gmail.com
www.itsgigisworldbooks.com
www.facebook.com/itsgigisworldbooks

God Made It

ISBN: 13: 978-0-9992624-1-2

Printed in the United States of America.

For bulk purchases and discounts for nonprofit organizations, contact It's GiGi's World Books, LLC at itsgigisworldbooks@gmail.com.

This book is dedicated to:

Walt, Steph, Kim, Sharifa and Kailah

You are my rock and my biggest
supporters! Love you guys!!!

Special thanks to:

E. Danielle Butler
for being the wind beneath my wings.
I could not have done this without you!

and

Pastor Daniel Perry (Pastor "P") for his insight and
reminder to always push for excellence.

∞

To God be the Glory and Honor for His
inspiration for this book.

The Birth of "God Made It"

During the summer of 2017, I had the opportunity to work with a group of 5-year-olds in summer camp. Crafting was something I've always dabbled in, so I enthusiastically accepted the challenge to take on the craft portion for the "Study of Creation."

And, oh my, did we have fun! What evolved was a different craft for each day of creation. Glue, colored papers, crayons, yarn and scissors were in full operation!
As the children and I talked throughout the crafting, it occurred to me that they were mixing up the order of creation. So I thought, "How can I get them to remember what God created first?"

Then, one night as I continued to pondered a resolve, God gave me lyrics. Grabbing paper and pen (yes, in that order), I hastily wrote them down!

Over the remainder of summer camp we sang these lyrics to a tune and incorporated hip-hop rhythms from the minds and mouths of preschoolers. Using our hands to clap and our feet to stomp, we created beats that breathed life into the sequence of God's creation which came to life. And, the best part was yelling "YUCK!"

Your children will have fun reading the lyrics that accompany vibrant illustrations. This story of Genesis will take on new meaning in their hearts that will extend a lifetime.

His,

Roz

Day One, He divided
the dark and light.

And, it was good in His sight.

Day Two, He made
the atmosphere.

Then, the heavens
and sky appeared.

Day Three, He gathered
the waters from the land.

That's when the trees
and the plants began.

Day Four, He created
two great lights.

The sun and the moon, then
the stars shined bright!

The birds and the fish,
He made on Day Five.

He said,
"Be fruitful and multiply!"

Day Six, was a busy
time; making living
creatures after its kind.

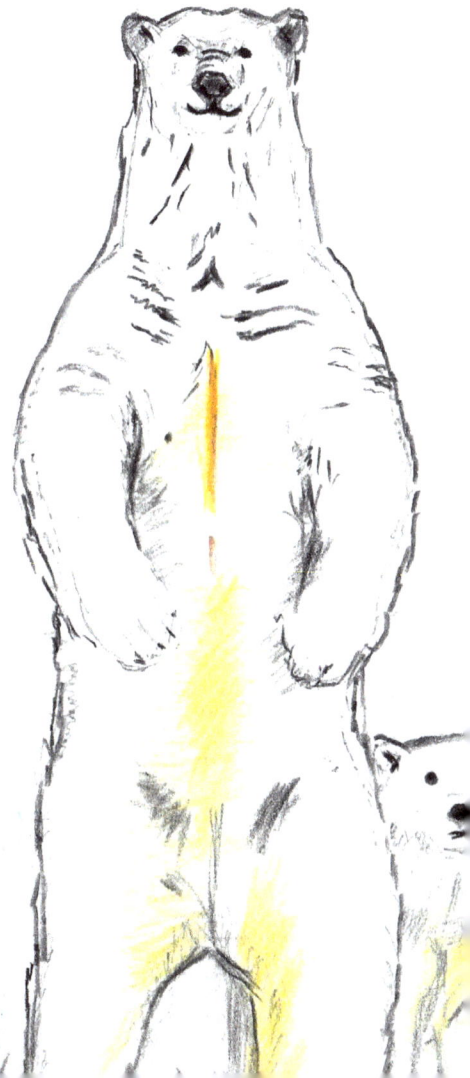

Like dogs and cats that
walk on the ground;
even bugs that creep,
"yuck!" they make
us frown.

Also, on Day Six,
He created man;

to take care of
everything was His plan.

With everything done
by the seventh day;

zzZ...

it was time to rest
from what He had made.

Then, He blessed that day and made it Holy!

And, we must always
remember this story.

We give God thanks
for everything!

To Him, our worship
is what we bring.

Our God is awesome
and we will tell;

everyone
who
listens,
"It is well!"

God Made It

Introducing your child to God's Word at a young age is exciting and fun. Below are some ways to use this book.

Younger Children:
Speak the words of this rhyme lyrically and clapped your hands to a beat that make the words come to life.
(Ps. 98:5)

For little kids, each page contains pictures that they can point to and talk about. They can count the number of fish, count the animals and talk about the bugs – Yuck!!
Discuss why God made them all different.
(1 Cor. 15:39)

Older Children:
Did you realize that the plants were created before the sun? God's light provided everything needed for photosynthesis to occur!
(Rev 21:23)

The animals are from several continents. A great opportunity to discuss why it is important that God's people inhabit each continent. (Acts 17:26; Ps. 22:27)

On the page about worship, ask "Why is a heart depicted?"
Good opportunity to discuss having a heart for God. (Ps. 86:12)

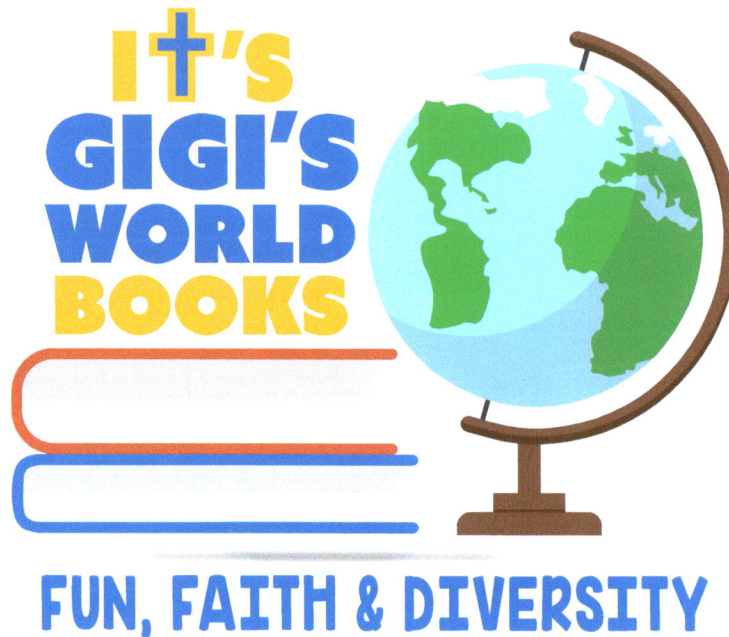

I†'S GIGI'S WORLD BOOKS

FUN, FAITH & DIVERSITY

Teaching support materials are available for this book at
www.itsgigisworldbooks.com.

The activities are designed for parents, home schoolers and children's ministries. Resources include coloring pages, discussion questions and lesson plans with supporting crafts for each day of creation.

Rosalind Bennett developed a passion for writing after retiring from the corporate world. With the ability to devote time in volunteering with several bible-based children's ministries, the mission of making God's Word engaging yet memorable for little ones has been her focus.

Rosalind created supplemental materials to use with various children's ministries. These materials created a layered approach to teaching God's Word and the Bible stories.

"It's Gigi's World Books" is a way to share these materials and resources with others who have the same passion for sharing their faith and teaching children.

Jonathan Barnhill is an illustrator with a love for drawing and fine arts. He began sketching at a very young age and continued developing his skills through high school. His gift was primarily shared through sketching for family and friends.

After leaving his sketch pad for a number of years, he found himself rediscovering his love of drawing again.

Jonathan resides in Atlanta, GA with his wife and two children. You can reach out to him at jbsketchez@gmail.com.

www.ingramcontent.com/pod-product-compliance
Lightning Source LLC
Chambersburg PA
CBHW040231070426
42447CB00030B/125